Word Problems
GRADE 8

Written by
Anne L. Steele

Illustrated by
Daisy dePuthod

Cover Illustration
by Susan Cumbow

FS-12012 Word Problems Grade 8
All rights reserved—Printed in the U.S.A.

Copyright © 1998 Frank Schaffer Publications, Inc.
23740 Hawthorne Blvd.
Torrance, CA 90505

TABLE OF CONTENTS

Introduction 2

Growing Produce (Whole number operations) 3

Computer Supplies (Reviewing decimals) 4

The Costumes (Adding and subtracting fractions) 5

Setting the Stage (Multiplying and dividing fractions) 6

What's the Expression? (Writing addition and subtraction expressions) 7

School Clubs (Addition and subtraction equations) 8

Vacation Travel (Multiplication and division equations) 9

Furniture Shopping (Two-step equations) 10

Temperature Fun (Adding and subtracting integers) 11

The Football Game (Multiplying and dividing integers) 12

The Integer Game (Reviewing integers) 13

Stock Exchange (Adding and subtracting rational numbers) 14

Let's Exercise (Multiplying and dividing rational numbers) 15

What's the Rate? (Solving rate problems) 16

Find the Bargain (Finding unit prices) 17

Planning a Party (Solving proportions) 18

What's the Discount? (Finding a percent of a number) 19

What's the Number? (Finding a number when a percent of it is known) 20

Finding Percentages (Finding the percent one number is of another) 21

Fun with Interest (Using interest) 22

Gardening All Around (Finding perimeter and circumference) 23

The Carpet Store (Finding areas) 24

Wrapping Presents (Finding the surface area) 25

Name the Volume (Finding the volume) 26

It's Probably There (Finding the probability) 27

Weather Watch (Predicting with probability) 28

How Many Ways? (Permutations and combinations) 29

Student Fun (Finding the mean, median, and mode) 30

Answers 31–32

Notice! Student pages may be reproduced by the classroom teacher for classroom use only, not for commercial resale. No part of this publication may be reproduced for storage in a retrieval system, or transmitted in any form or by any means—electronic, mechanical, recording, etc.—without the prior written permission of the publisher. Reproduction of these materials for an entire school or school system is strictly prohibited.

INTRODUCTION

This book has been designed to help students succeed in math. It is part of the *Math Minders* series, which provides students with opportunities to practice math skills through word problems.

The activities in the book have been created to help students feel confident about solving word problems. The format of the book begins with a review of skills learned in earlier grades and moves gradually to skills introduced and developed in eighth grade. The activities are developed to give the students an opportunity to meet with both success and challenge in working with word problems. Each activity features a theme to help maintain a high level of interest as students complete it . The activities can be used as supplemental material to reinforce any existing math program.

The skills covered in the book can be taught in the classroom or at home. They include addition, subtraction, multiplication, and division of whole numbers, decimals, fractions, integers, and rational numbers; writing and solving equations; percents; probability; and much more.

Word Problems GRADE 8

Name_____

Solve each problem.

A. The Palma family owned a farm. One year they grew 1,150 acres of soybeans for the spring, 6,450 acres of soybeans for the summer, and 4,985 acres of soybeans for the fall. What was the total acreage of soybeans that the Palma family grew?

_____

B. One year Vlad decided to grow cantaloupe and honeydew. He produced 15,161 tons of cantaloupe and 8,957 tons of honeydew. How many more tons of cantaloupe did Vlad produce than honeydew?

_____

C. On Fridays, Hazel took some of the produce to the farmers' market. The truck carried 195 bushels of produce. Hazel went to the farmers' market 15 Fridays, each time taking a full truck of produce. How many bushels did she take to the farmer's market altogether?

_____

D. Dee picked 672 flowers from her garden. She arranged the flowers into bouquets. Each bouquet had 21 flowers. How many bouquets did Dee make?

_____

E. John grew 148,512 pints of strawberries. To carry the strawberries to market, the pints were put on wooden flats. If 12 pints fit on one flat, how many flats did John need?

_____

F. Chris decided to grow asparagus for spring and summer produce. He produced 386,547 tons of asparagus in the spring and 127,226 tons in the summer. How much asparagus did he produce in all?

_____

G. Emily was considering growing tomatoes the next year. She was told that an acre of tomatoes produces 205 bushels of tomatoes. If she were to plant 2,754 acres of tomatoes, how many bushels would she produce?

_____

Name_____

Solve each problem.

A. A printer costs $289.95. It is on sale for $25.00 off the original price. What is the sale price of the printer?

_____

B. Ida buys a computer system for $1,299.99, word-processing software for $634.87, and a conversion program for $75.65. What is the total amount Ida spends?

_____

C. Scottwood School uses 876 cases of paper per year. A case of paper costs $47.88. What is the cost of the paper for the year?

_____

D. Rick buys a carrying case for his computer notebook. He saves $15.99 by buying it on sale for $63.96. What is the regular price of the carrying case?

_____

E. Libbie can buy a package of 50 disks for $14.50. What would be the cost of one disk?

_____

F. Jill needs to purchase paper. A ream of paper costs $3.99. How much would 12 reams of paper cost?

_____

G. Curtis buys a computer stand for $239.95. He also buys a new desk chair for $157.35. Curtis gives the clerk $400.00. How much change will Curtis get back?

_____

H. Howard buys 9 ink cartridges for $211.50. What is the cost of one ink cartridge?

_____

Name ______________________________

THE COSTUMES

Adding and subtracting fractions

Wickfield School was having a school play, and the costumes needed to be made. Solve each problem.

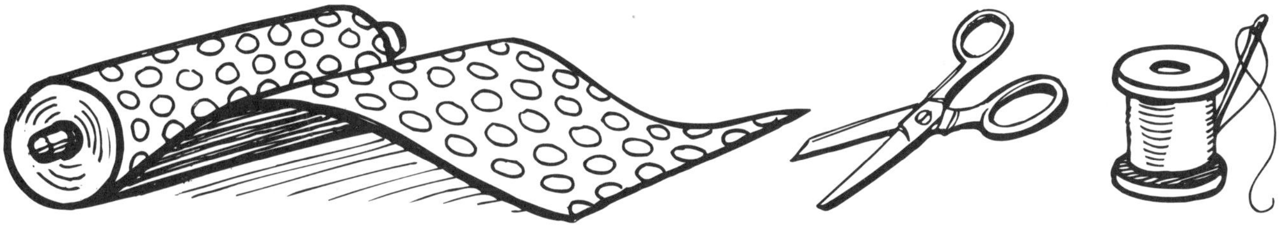

A. Stephanie needed $8\frac{1}{3}$ yards of blue polka-dotted fabric for her costume. The fabric store only had $5\frac{1}{6}$ yards of the fabric that she needed. How much material did Stephanie still need for her costume?

____

B. Anita bought 13 yards of fabric for her costume. After cutting out the costume, she had $3\frac{5}{8}$ yards left over. How much fabric did she use to make her costume?

____

C. Ben had two parts in the play, so, he had to make two costumes. The clown costume took $8\frac{5}{8}$ yards of fabric, and the lion tamer costume took $14\frac{1}{2}$ yards of fabric. How much fabric did Ben need in all?

____

D. Lisa needed $12\frac{5}{8}$ yards of purple silk for the skirt of her costume and $6\frac{1}{16}$ yards of white cotton for the top of her costume. What was the total number of yards of fabric that Lisa needed?

____

E. Lisa went to Nelson's Fabric Store to purchase the $12\frac{5}{8}$ yards of purple silk. The bolt had $39\frac{2}{3}$ yards of fabric before Lisa bought her material. How many yards of fabric were on the bolt after Lisa purchased her material?

____

F. Clifford's mother had to take his measurements before purchasing the material. She measured $28\frac{3}{4}$ inches for his inseam and $19\frac{7}{5}$ inches for his torso. How much longer was his inseam than his torso?

____

G. Kathy needed $2\frac{1}{5}$ yards of black material for her hat and $13\frac{2}{10}$ yards of black material for her jacket. How many yards of black material did Kathy need for her costume?

____

© Frank Schaffer Publications, Inc.

Name_____

The set and props needed to be built or set up for the Wickfield School play. Solve each problem.

A. Stephen laid 3 pieces of wood side-by-side to build a bench. Each piece of wood was 16⅔ inches wide. How wide was the bench?

_____

B. Among the props to be built were a tree and a flower. The tree needed to be 6½ feet tall, and the flower needed to be 2⅔ feet tall. How many times the flower's height was the tree's height?

_____

C. The students had to buy rope for the curtain. The cost of the rope was 32¢ a foot. What was the cost of 14¼ feet of rope?

_____

D. The lighting crew needed to place the lights along the front of the stage, which was 16 feet wide. The lights were 1⅛ feet wide. How many lights were used?

_____

E. Stacey built a screen that had 3 sections. Each section was 16⅔ inches wide. How wide was the entire screen?

_____

F. Tina had to build a birdhouse for the props. She had a 6-foot board. She needed to cut ½-foot pieces from this board. How many pieces did she cut from this board?

_____

G. The art crew needed to paint a mural that covered ⅔ of the length of the back wall and 8/12 of the height of the back wall. What part of the whole wall was covered by the mural?

_____

H. The stage crew needed to place a row of stools along the counter of a restaurant. The stools were 1½ feet wide. How many stools were placed along the counter, which was 4⅛ feet long?

_____

Name_____

Write an expression for each problem.

A. Bill scored x field goals in last weekend's basketball game. He made 4 more free throws than field goals. What expression represents the number of free throws?

_____

B. Bill and Cynthia scored a total of 62 points. Bill scored y of these points. What expression shows the points for Cynthia?

_____

C. The Panthers have played 15 games so far this season. They won w of the games. What expression represents the number of games they lost this season?

_____

D. The Cougars play 82 games in a basketball season. There were x games played away, and the remainder were home games. What expression represents the number of home games?

_____

E. Stacey's baseball team played x games this season. Patty's team played 15 more games than Stacey's team. What expression represents the number of games Patty's team played?

_____

F. Kelly scored y goals in soccer this month. She had 19 more assists than goals this month. What expression represents the number of assists?

_____

G. Naz ran 5 times farther during the month of July than Mark. What is an expression for the distance Naz ran?

_____

H. The Bears bought 65 new tennis balls, and there were x players. What is an expression for the number of balls each player had?

_____

I. Kari made 4 times as many free throws as Kurt at their game last Friday. What is an expression for the number of free throws Kari made?

_____

J. There were 25 football players on the team. Every player made the same number of touchdowns. The team made y touchdowns. What is an expression for the number of touchdowns each player made?

_____

K. Scott threw the javelin 3 times farther than Daniel threw the javelin. What is an expression for the distance Scott threw the javelin?

_____

© Frank Schaffer Publications, Inc.
FS-12012 Word Problems Grade 8

Name_____

Write and solve an equation for each problem.

A Two after-school clubs met on Monday, the Glee Club and the Art Club. A total of 78 students were members of the Monday clubs. The Art Club had 33 students. How many students were in the Glee Club?

_____

B. Victor asked Mr. Smithers, the drama teacher, how many students were in the Drama Club. Mr. Smithers said, "If 21 students were subtracted from the number of students in the Drama Club, the difference would be the number of students in the Math Club." Victor knew that there were 80 students in the Math Club because he was a member. How many students were in the Drama Club?

_____

C. Sally knew that there were 23 students in the orchestra. However, she wanted to send holiday cards to every student in the band. Mr. Sowle told her that there were 4 more students in the orchestra than the band. How many students were in the band?

_____

D. Todd wanted to give everyone in the Dance Club a treat. Mrs. Hamblett told him that the Speech Club had 182 students less than the Dance Club. Todd knew there were 144 students in the Speech Club. How many students were in the Dance Club?

_____

E. Philip wanted to know how many students were in the Reading Club. Ms. Spino said, "If 70 students were added to the number of students in the Reading Club, the total would be the same as the number of students in the Environmental Club." Philip knew that there were 214 students in the Environmental Club. How many students were in the Reading Club?

_____

F. The Spanish Club and the German Club were trying to raise money to help children. They decided to sell candy. They raised $125 more than what they raised last year. Last year they raised $950 dollars. How much did they raise this year?

_____

Name_____

Many of the students at Riverdale traveled over summer vacation. They recorded some facts about their travels. Write and solve the equation for each problem.

A. Mickey and Becky drove to visit relatives all over the country. They drove 5,599 miles in 11 weeks. If they traveled the same distance each week, how far did they travel per week?

_____

B. Wendy took the train to her grandmother's house. The train traveled an average of 3 miles per hour because it made many stops. Wendy rode on the train for 72 hours. What distance did Wendy travel?

_____

C. Susanne spent the summer at her aunt's house. Susanne drove 156 miles to get there. This is 12 times farther than Kari traveled on her trip to her uncle's house. How far did Kari travel?

_____

D. Ralph walked to visit friends. He walked 2.5 miles per day. How far did Ralph travel in 60 days?

_____

E. Tia flew with her father, who is an airline pilot. Tia flew 11,200 miles in one week. How many miles did she average per day?

_____

F. Mia took a bus to Tucson, which took 4 days. The total distance she traveled was 640 miles. How far did she travel per day if the bus traveled the same distance each day?

_____

G. Peter bicycled through Colorado during the summer. He traveled to 12 places. If he traveled 60 miles to each place, how many miles did he travel altogether?

_____

H. Elizabeth drove 175 miles on her vacation, and Clint drove 700 miles on his vacation. Clint's distance was how many times Elizabeth's distance?

_____

Name_____

Brenda's mother was considering buying new household goods. She asked Brenda to go shopping with her to help figure out the costs. Write and solve an equation for each problem.

A. While riding in the car, Brenda decided to practice her math skills. She asked her mother to give her a problem. Her mother said, "A certain number is multiplied by 2, and 4 is added to the product. The total is 20. What is the number?"

_____

B. "That was fun!" said Brenda. "Give me one more." Her mother said, "Here's one. When 2 is subtracted from the quotient of a number divided by 11, the difference is 1. What is the number?"

_____

C. Brenda and her mother arrived at the store. Her mother found some place mats for the kitchen table. She gave Brenda $20 to pay for the place mats. Brenda bought 3 place mats and received $2 back. How much did each place mat cost?

_____

D. Brenda's mother found some living room furniture. The total cost with tax and interest was $2,250. Brenda's mother asked her to figure how much each payment would be if she made a down payment of $450 and paid off the balance in 8 equal payments. How much was each payment?

_____

E. As they were walking through the store, Brenda saw a picture for her bedroom. The price of the picture was $145. Brenda wanted to buy the picture, but she had only $25. Brenda thought, "How much must I save each week in order to have $145 at the end of 8 weeks?"

_____

F. Brenda's mother saw some candlesticks. She had a coupon for $25 off one candlestick. She used the coupon and bought 6 candlesticks for a total of $227. Brenda's mother asked, "Brenda, what is the cost of each candlestick without the coupon?"

_____

G. As they were leaving the store, Brenda's mother saw some picture frames. She thought they would make nice birthday gifts, so she bought 7 frames for a total of $47, including tax. Brenda's mother asked, "If the tax was $5, what was the cost of each frame without tax?"

_____

Name_____

During the winter, Keith kept a record of the temperatures for a week. Help Keith solve each problem.

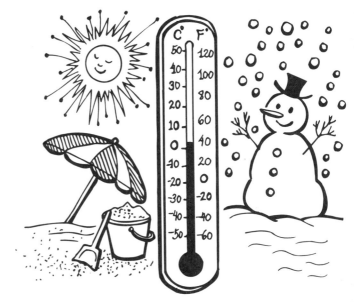

A. On Sunday morning, the temperature was ⁻4° F. On Sunday afternoon, the temperature was ⁻9° F. What was the difference between the temperatures?

_____

B. On Monday, the temperature in the morning was ⁻16° F. By lunchtime, the temperature had risen 12°. What was the temperature at lunchtime?

_____

C. On Tuesday, the high temperature was 15° F. At night, the temperature dropped 21° from the high. What was the temperature at night?

_____

D. On Thursday morning, the temperature was ⁻4° F. By the afternoon, the temperature had dropped ⁻6°. What was the afternoon temperature?

_____

E. On Friday, the afternoon temperature was 9° F. By the evening, the temperature had dropped to ⁻11° F. How many degrees did the temperature drop?

_____

F. On Saturday, the afternoon temperature was ⁻9° F. By the evening, the temperature was 8° warmer. What was the temperature by the evening?

_____

G. The lowest recorded temperature during this week of January was ⁻22° F. The highest recorded temperature was 32° F. What was the difference between the temperatures?

_____

THE FOOTBALL GAME ....

The Cougars were competing against the Tigers in football. Carl attended the game and kept records of the yardage gained and lost on certain plays. Help Carl solve each problem. Use negative numbers for losses and positive numbers for gains.

A. In the past 5 plays, the Cougars have received a 5-yard penalty on each play. By how many yards did the Cougars' position on the field change?

_____

B. During the game, the Tigers received 8 penalty violations for a total loss of 40 yards. If they lost the same yardage for each penalty call, by how many yards did the Tigers' field position change on each penalty?

_____

C. The Cougars' quarterback was sacked on the last 3 plays. The team lost 16 yards each time the quarterback was sacked. How many yards ahead were the Cougars 3 plays ago?

_____

D. The Tigers lost 50 yards on penalty violations in 5 plays. If they lost the same yardage each time, by how many yards did the Tigers' field position change?

_____

E. The Tigers' quarterback was sacked 6 times during the game. Each time, the team lost 8 yards. By how many yards did the Tigers' total yardage change because of quarterback sacks?

_____

F. The Cougars' running back lost 9 yards on each of the last 4 plays. How many yards ahead were the Cougars 4 plays ago?

_____

G. The Tigers have lost a total of 85 yards in 17 plays. By how many yards did the Tigers' field position change on each play if they lost the same yardage each time?

_____

Name_____

The students in Mrs. Clark's class were playing the integer game. Help the students write and solve an equation for each problem.

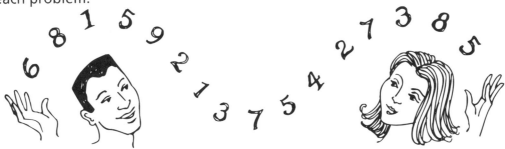

A. Greg said, "I thought of an integer. I multiplied it by 6, and the product was ⁻18." What was Greg's integer?

_____

B. Zak said, "I thought of an integer. I divided it by ⁻13. The quotient was ⁻4." What was Zak's integer?

_____

C. Rhonda said, "I added ⁻4 to my integer and got ⁻7 as the sum." What was Rhonda's integer?

_____

D. Brian said, "If you added ⁻13 to my year of birth, the sum would be 1972." What was Brian's integer?

_____

E. Monica said, "If you multiplied my integer by 8, you would get ⁻72." What was Monica's integer?

_____

F. Jacob said, "I subtracted ⁻5 from my integer and got ⁻5." What was Jacob's integer?

_____

G. Lewellyn said, "I thought of an integer. I divided it by 2. The quotient was ⁻19." What was Lewellyn's integer?

_____

Name_____

Solve each problem.

A. Mike's father owned some shares of computer stock. The change in the price of a share of stock was $-\frac{3}{8}$ one day. The next day, the change was $+\frac{3}{4}$. What was the total change in price for the two days?

_____

B. Meredith's mother owned some shares of toy store stock. The stock was selling for $37\frac{5}{8} a share at the beginning of the day. At the end of the day, it was selling for $24\frac{3}{8} a share. How much did the price of a share drop from the beginning of the day to the end of the day?

_____

C. Mark's father owned some shares of ice cream stock. The price of a share of stock closed "up" $7\frac{3}{16}$ on Thursday. The stock closed "down" $4\frac{1}{16}$ on Friday. What was the total change in the price for the two days?

_____

D. Millie's aunt was thinking about buying some shares of stock. The stock of a telephone company was selling for $37\frac{1}{2} a share. The stock of an airline company was selling for $14\frac{15}{16} a share. How much more did one share of the telephone company stock cost?

_____

E. Marvin's uncle owned some shares of automobile stock. The stock closed at $-\frac{8}{10}$ on Monday. On Tuesday, the stock closed at $-\frac{3}{5}$. What was the total change in price of the stock for the two days?

_____

F. Marilyn's aunt owned some shares of a movie company's stock. On Tuesday, the stock closed at $-\frac{1}{8}$. Marilyn's uncle owned some shares of a theater's stock. On Tuesday, the stock closed at $-\frac{7}{8}$. What was the difference between the two drops in the stocks?

_____

Name_____

Many of the students' parents were exercising. They were keeping records of their weight gains and losses. Solve each problem. Use negative numbers for losses and positive numbers for gains.

A. Joseph's father wanted to lose 3.4 pounds per week over 21 weeks by biking. How much total weight did Joseph's father want to lose?

_____

B. Amy's mother lost 9.25 pounds in the last 5⅕ weeks by rowing and lifting weights. What was her mother's average loss in weight per week?

_____

C. Jennifer's father wanted to lose 2½ pounds in a week. He planned to eat healthfully and walk. He was able to lose only ⅘ of that amount. How many pounds did Jennifer's father lose?

_____

D. Maria's mother lost 12 pounds in 2⅓ months by eating healthfully and playing tennis. What was her mother's average loss in weight per month?

_____

E. Jack's father planned to lose ¾ of a pound per week over 4 weeks by running. How much weight did Jack's father want to lose altogether?

_____

F. Jude's mother gained 1¾ pounds the first week, lost 2 pounds the next week, and gained 1½ pounds the next week. What was his mother's average gain or loss in weight per week?

_____

G. Jeffrey's father wanted to lose 5.6 pounds in two weeks. He planned on playing racqetball to lose the weight. At the end of two weeks, he lost only ⅜ of that amount. How many pounds did Jeffrey's father lose?

_____

© Frank Schaffer Publications, Inc.

Name_____

WHAT'S THE RATE? ....

The students in Mr. Kentra's class were playing the "Name the Rate Game." Each student made up a problem, and the other students answered. Help the class solve each problem.

A. Harry said, "The basketball team needed to raise money for new uniforms. They decided to earn money by mowing lawns. They charged $12 for a job that took 4 hours. What was their rate per hour?"

_____

B. Maureen said, "I have been taking typing lessons. Now I can type 225 words in 5 minutes. What is my typing rate in words per minute?"

_____

C. Nadja said, "I needed to earn money to buy a birthday gift for my mother. I decided to baby-sit for my neighbors, the Smiths. I charged the Smiths $7 for 4 hours. What was my hourly rate?"

_____

D. Tasha said, "I was saving money to purchase a new bicycle. I washed windows in my neighborhood. I charged $2.75 an hour. It took me 3.2 hours to wash the Simpsons' windows. What did I charge the Simpsons?"

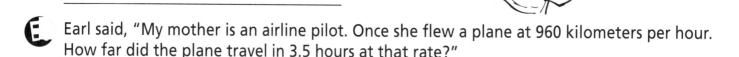

_____

E. Earl said, "My mother is an airline pilot. Once she flew a plane at 960 kilometers per hour. How far did the plane travel in 3.5 hours at that rate?"

_____

F. Valerie said, "I was thirsty, so I went to the store to buy some juice. I paid $2.96 for an 8-liter bottle. What was the rate per liter?"

_____

G. Oliver said, "I like reading books. Once I read a book in 5 hours. The book was 275 pages long. What was my reading rate in pages per hour?"

_____

H. Cleo said, "My older brother is in college. He is in class for 384 minutes and is taking 6 classes. How many minutes is one class?"

_____

Name_____

Erin's family were bargain shoppers. On Friday, they went shopping. Help Erin's family find the bargain.
Solve each problem.

A. Erin's mother needed to purchase stationery. She saw a box of 12 cards with a seashell
design for $3.96 and a box of 8 cards with a floral design for $2.96. What was the unit
price of each item? Which cards were the better bargain?

_____

B. Erin's father needed to purchase videotapes. He saw two signs: "Top Quality Tapes—5 for
$14.85" and "Great Quality Tapes—3 for $8.85." What was the unit price of each item?
Which tapes were the better bargain?

_____

C. Erin's grandfather needed to purchase prune juice. He checked the prices. A 32-ounce
bottle cost $1.69 and a 64-ounce bottle cost $2.79. What was the unit price of each item?
Which bottle was the better bargain?

_____

D. Erin's sister needed to buy some perfume for a birthday gift. The 1.5-fluid-ounce bottle
cost $43.95. The 3-fluid-ounce bottle cost $88.98. What was the unit price of each item?
Which bottle was the better bargain?

_____

E. Erin's brother needed new socks for track. When he walked into the sporting goods store,
he saw a sign: "Sock Sale— 3 for $7.62." As he was about to pay for the socks, he noticed
another sign: "New Track Socks— 2 for $5.28." What was the unit price of each item?
Which was the better bargain?

_____

F. Erin needed to buy some cat food for her cat, Sneakers. The price for 5 cans was $1.55 and
the price for 3 cans was $0.99. What was the unit price of each item? Which was the
better bargain?

_____

Name_____

Teagan is planning a surprise party for her parents. Help Teagan write and solve a proportion for each problem.

A. Teagan invited 100 people to a party last year, and 37 people did not attend. If Teagan invites 215 people this year, about how many people will not attend the party?

_____

B. Teagan has to mix the punch for the party. She pours 15 gallons of water into a bowl. How many cups of punch mix should she add to the water if it takes 2 cups of punch mix for every 3 gallons of water?

_____

C. Teagan needs to purchase 100 more invitations for the party. If there are 13 invitations in one box, how many boxes will Teagan need to purchase?

_____

D. Teagan needs to buy flowers for the tables. The florist has a special— 2 bouquets for $5. If Teagan pays the florist $27.50 for the flowers, how many bouquets will Teagan purchase?

_____

E. Teagan wonders how much chocolate cake she should make. She takes a poll and finds that 5 out of 8 people like chocolate cake. If there are 200 people at the party, how many of them may want chocolate cake?

_____

F. Teagan sees an ad in the newspaper: "Ice Cream—4 Half-Gallons for $9.00." If Teagan purchases 10 half-gallons of ice cream, how much will she pay?

_____

Name_____

Esther wanted to practice finding a percent of a number. She went to the mall to look for sales. Help Esther find the discount.

A. First Esther went to the bike shop. She saw a sale sign: "15% Off All Bikes." Esther found a bike in her favorite color, red. The regular price of the bike was $320. What was the discount?

_____

B. Esther went to the shoe store. She looked at the running shoes. She found a pair with green stripes for 40% off the regular price of $90. What was the discount?

_____

C. The salesperson told Esther that all clothing was 25% off. Esther looked at the jogging suits. She found a suit that would match the shoes. The regular price was $125. What was the discount?

_____

D. Next, Esther walked into a clothing shop. She looked at some beautiful sweaters. All sweaters were 30% off the regular price. Esther found a purple wool sweater for $65. What was the discount?

_____

E. Esther looked for a skirt to match the purple sweater. She found a gorgeous floral skirt for $45. The salesperson told Esther that all skirts were 10% off. What was the discount?

_____

F. Esther left the clothing shop and kept looking for sales signs. She saw a large sale sign outside the pet shop. Esther was excited. She loved animals. Esther entered the store and saw a golden retriever puppy for $530. The sale was offering 55% off all dogs. What was the discount?

_____

G. Then Esther saw a white kitten playing with a ball of yarn. Esther asked the salesperson the price. It was $245, with 35% off. What was the discount?

_____

Name_____

Several students have a newspaper route. Write and solve an equation for each problem.

A. Daryl delivers the Sunday newspaper to 25% of his customers. There are 32 customers who receive the Sunday paper. How many customers does Daryl have?

_____

B. Lucille delivers the weekend newspapers to 50% of her customers. There are 190 customers who do not receive the weekend newspapers. How many customers does Lucille have?

_____

C. There are 65% of Vickie's customers who pay for the newspaper on a monthly basis, or 130 customers who pay monthly. How many customers does Vickie have?

_____

D. Mr. French's company pays for 30% of the cost of his newspaper. The company pays $90 a year. What is the total annual cost of the newspaper?

_____

E. Logan delivers the newspapers to offices and homes. There are 35% of his customers who receive their papers at home, or 21 customers who receive papers at home. How many customers does Logan have?

_____

F. Janet delivers the early edition newspaper to 7% of her customers. There are 42 customers who receive the early edition newspaper. How many customers does Janet have?

_____

Name_____

Many of the students at McCord School were involved in extracurricular activities. Help the students find the percentage.

A. Rachel played on the volleyball team. She served 9 aces out of 20 serves. What percent of serves were aces?

_____

B. Eli was on the spelling team. To compete in the regional meet, he had to get 20 spelling words correct. He got 45 spelling words correct. What percent of the number required were the number he got correct?

_____

C. Barbara got 78 out of 90 questions correct in the math competition on Saturday. What percent of questions did Barbara get correct?

_____

D. The Chess Team needed 15 more points to make it to the state competition. The team scored 75 points. What percent of the points needed was the points scored?

_____

E. Todd was on the basketball team. He made 12 free throws out of 22 attempts. What percent of free throws did Todd make?

_____

F. Freddy was on the debate team. The team scored a total of 65 points. Freddy contributed 13 points. What percent of the total points did Freddy score?

_____

G. Dawn played on the soccer team. She attempted 30 goals and made 21 goals for the season. What percent of goals did she make?

_____

H. Ralph played on the basketball team. At the end of the season, the team had 325 rebounds. Ralph had a total of 65 rebounds at the end of the season. What percent of the total rebounds did Ralph have?

_____

© Frank Schaffer Publications, Inc.

Name_____

Keith's family needs help keeping track of their finances. Help Keith's family solve the problems.

 A. Keith's older brother borrowed $4,000 to pay for a new sports car. The loan was for 3 years. The interest rate was 14% per year. What was the interest he had to pay?

_____

B. Keith's sister went to college. She took out a loan of $7,500 for tuition. The loan was for 5 years with an interest rate of 8.25% per year. What was the interest? What was the total amount she had to repay?

_____

 **C.** Keith's younger brother saved his money. He put $4,325 in a money market fund 5 years ago. The interest rate on the account was 14% per year. How much interest did he earn?

_____

D. Keith's mother won $1,320 in the lottery. She decided to put the money in her IRA, which would earn 12% per year. How much interest did she earn in 6 years and 6 months?

_____

E. Keith's father needed a new sail for his boat. He bought an $800 sail using his credit card. The interest rate was 18% per year. If Keith's father paid off the bill in 3 months, what was the interest he had to pay? What was the total amount he paid?

_____

F. Keith's grandfather had $500 in a savings account for the last 10 years with an interest rate of 4% per year. He wanted to use the interest to purchase a new bicycle. How much money did he have to spend on a new bicycle?

_____

G. Keith earned $625 over the summer being a caddy. He put this money in a money market fund with an interest rate of 12.25% per year. If Keith left the money in the fund for 6 months, how much money did he have at the end of those 6 months?

_____

Name_____

Yitzi's father was a gardener. During the summer, Yitzi worked with his father. Help Yitzi solve each problem.

A. Mrs. Rodriguez wanted azalea bushes planted around the perimeter of her yard. Yitzi and his father measured the length and width of the yard. The length was 41 feet, and the width was 25.5 feet. Yitzi made a sketch for his father. What was the perimeter of Mrs. Rodriguez's yard?

_____

B. The Wilsons wanted impatiens planted around their patio. Yitzi measured and drew a sketch of the patio while his father was trimming the trees. What was the perimeter of the patio?

_____

C. Mrs. Simmons wanted to have pansies planted around the oak tree in her front yard. Yitzi's father needed the circumference of the tree to know how many pansies to buy. Yitzi measured the diameter of the tree, which was 75 centimeters. What was the circumference of the tree?

_____

D. The Steinmans wanted to fence in the corner of their backyard to make a garden. They asked Yitzi's father if he could build a picket fence to form a triangular area. Yitzi and his father measured and made the following sketch. What was the perimeter of the garden?

_____

E. Mr. Thomas wanted to have some daisies planted around the wishing well in his backyard. Yitzi knew his father would need the circumference of the wishing well, so he measured the radius of it. The radius was 18 inches. What was the circumference of the wishing well?

_____

F. The Morgans had a sandbox in the shape of a parallelogram. They needed to replace the wood around the sandbox. Yitzi's father said he could replace it for them. How many feet of wood were needed to go around the sandbox, which was 5.5 feet wide and 7 feet long?

_____

Name_____

The Wagners own a carpet store. Help the Wagners solve each problem.

A. Billy is redecorating his bedroom. He wants to recarpet the room, which is square with an area of 169 square feet. What is the length of each side of the bedroom?

_____

B. Danny is putting new carpeting in the Smiths' living room. The rectangular room has a length of 16 feet and a width of 12 feet. How many square feet of carpeting are needed to cover the Smiths' living room?

_____

C. Mrs. Graham comes into the carpet store to look for carpet for her foyer. The dimensions of the foyer are 3.5 feet wide and 4.8 feet long. Cheryl shows her various samples of carpet. Mrs. Graham likes the dark blue carpet at $13.99 per square foot. What is the area of Mrs. Graham's foyer? What is the cost of the blue carpet for this area?

_____

D. Ms. Foist comes into the carpet store looking for a circular rug with a diameter of 10 feet for her classroom. The carpet in the shop is only labeled by area. Robert must find the area of a circle with a diameter of 10 feet so he can show Ms. Foist the rugs. What is the area?

_____

E. The Skeans want a triangular piece of carpeting to go in the corner of their basement. Jennifer measures the corner and gets a base of 7.3 feet and a height of 8 feet. How many square feet of carpeting are needed to cover the corner?

_____

F. The Kleins are getting new carpet for their dining room. Leon arrives at the Kleins' house and notices that the shape of the dining room is a trapezoid. The parallel sides of the room measure 8 feet and 15 feet. The height is 7 feet. How many square feet of carpeting are needed to cover the Kleins' dining room?

_____

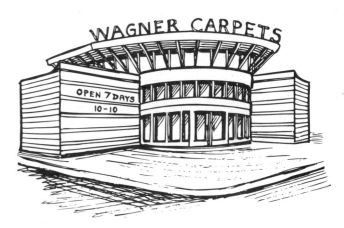

Name_____

WRAPPING PRESENTS·······

Gina and George were wrapping presents. They wanted to find the surface area of each box so they'd know how much paper to buy. Help Gina and George find the surface area of each box.

A. The first box was a gift for Gina and George's father. Inside it was a book. The box was a rectangular prism with a length of 8 inches, a width of 2 inches, and a height of 10 inches. What was the total surface area of this box?

_____

B. The next present was for their sister. It was a small crystal bowl. The box the present was wrapped in was a cube. Each side measured 20 cm. What was the total surface area of this box?

_____

C. Gina bought her mother a hat. The shape of the box was a cylinder. Gina measured the box. The radius was 12 inches, and the height was 8 inches. What was the total surface area of the hatbox?

_____

D. The next gift was a toy car for their brother. The box was a square pyramid. George measured the box. The height was 9.5 inches and the base was 5 inches. What was the total surface area of the box?

_____

E. The next gift was a ball for their younger brother. They decided to wrap the ball without using a box. George measured 4 centimeters as the radius of the ball. What was the total surface area of the ball?

_____

F. The next gift was for Uncle Phil. It was a small lamp. The box was cone-shaped with a radius of 2 inches and a height of 12 inches. What was the total surface area of the cone box?

_____

Name_____

Solve each problem.

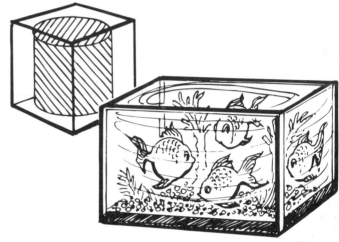

A. Peter puts a cylindrical candy jar with a diameter of 10 centimeters and a height of 10 centimeters inside a cube-shaped box that is 10.2 centimeters on each side. What is the volume of the part of the box not filled with the candy jar? Round to the nearest tenth.

_____

B. Jamie has a rectangular aquarium. He wants to figure out the volume before he begins to fill it with gravel and water. The aquarium has a length of 24 inches, a width of 12 inches, and a height of 14 inches. What is the volume of the aquarium?

_____

C. Sarah has a conical ice cream cone. She wants to fill the cone with ice cream. The cone has a diameter of 2 inches and a height of 5 inches. What is the volume of the ice cream cone? Round to the nearest whole number.

_____

D. Aunt Vickie is making applesauce. She buys cylindrical jars for the applesauce. The jars have a radius of 2.8 centimeters and a height of 11.6 centimeters. What is the volume of a jar? Round to the nearest cubic centimeter

_____

E. The truck that the McLean family uses to haul hay has a cargo space that is 1.3 meters high, 1.6 meters wide, and 2.5 meters long. What is the volume of the cargo space?

_____

Name_____

Burt and Bethany work at the athletics director's office at school. They help with the sports equipment. Help Burt and Bethany solve each problem.

A. Burt keeps various balls in a large wire basket. In the basket are 2 basketballs, 3 volleyballs, 5 soccer balls, and 1 football. If he were to reach into the basket without looking, what is the probability of Burt getting a . . .

football? _____   basketball? _____

volleyball? _____   soccer ball? _____

B. Sandy, the new girl at school, goes to the office to get a volleyball uniform. Bethany gets the duffel bag with the volleyball uniforms. On the side of the bag there is a note, "1 large shirt, 3 medium shirts, 5 small shirts, 2 large shorts, and 6 medium shorts." Sandy needs a medium shirt and large shorts. If Bethany were to reach into the duffel bag without looking, what is the probability of pulling out a . . .

medium shirt? _____   large shorts? _____

C. Some of the students want to purchase school sweatshirts. Burt keeps the sweatshirts in a trunk in the office. Currently, there are 4 blue sweatshirts, 7 red sweatshirts, 2 yellow sweatshirts, and 5 white sweatshirts. If he were to reach into the trunk without looking, what is the probability of Burt pulling out a . . .

red sweatshirt? _____   blue sweatshirt? _____

white sweatshirt? _____   yellow sweatshirt? _____

D. The athletic director wants to know how many of each color baseball cap is in the box. Bethany counts 3 blue caps, 9 red caps, and 6 white caps. Right after she finishes putting the caps into the box, Charles and Wanda walk into the office and ask Bethany if they can get a blue and a red baseball cap. If Bethany were to reach into the box without looking, what is the probability of pulling out a . . .

blue baseball cap? _____   red baseball cap? _____

E. Thomas walks into the office. He has ruined his football jersey, so he needs a new one. Burt gets the duffel bag containing the football uniforms. If Burt were to reach into the bag without looking, what is the probability of pulling out a jersey when there are 15 pants and 7 jerseys in the bag?

_____

Name_____

A meteorologist keeps records of weather conditions and can use these records to predict the possibility of storms or natural disasters. Use the information to solve each problem.

A. Mr. Edwards's records show that the probability of a tornado in the Midwest region of the United States on any day is about $\frac{1}{7}$. About how many tornadoes would be expected in this region in 365 days?

_____

B. Ms. Smith's records show that the probability of a rainy day in one year in her hometown is about $\frac{7}{9}$. About how many rainy days would be expected in 365 days?

_____

C. Mr. Tyler's records show that the probability of a hurricane in one year along the nearby coast is about $\frac{1}{36}$. About how many hurricanes would be expected in this region in 52 weeks?

_____

D. Mrs. Millare's records show that the probability of rain in Seattle during one year is about $\frac{2}{5}$. How many rainy days per year would be expected in Seattle?

_____

E. Mr. Burnham's records show that the probability of flooding in his city is $\frac{1}{60}$ during 180 days. How many floods in 180 days would be expected?

_____

F. Mr. Peterson's records show that the probability of a hurricane during a 6-month period in his county is about $\frac{1}{12}$. About how many hurricanes would be expected in his county in 6 months?

_____

G. Ms. Robertson's records show that the probability of a thunderstorm in her state during 84 days is about $\frac{1}{3}$. How many thunderstorms in 84 days would be expected?

_____

Name_____

Solve each problem.

A. Ted, Sarah, Ernest, and Kimberly are assigned to sit in 4 seats in a row. How many different seating arrangements are possible for the 4 students?

_____

B. Nick and Joyce are ordering a pizza for dinner. They have a coupon for 3 toppings. There are 5 toppings to choose from: olive, mushroom, pepperoni, green pepper, and sausage. How many different combinations of 3 toppings are possible?

_____

C. The students in Mr. Sweaner's class are writing reports. Mr. Sweaner gave the class a list of 5 topics to chose from: rain forest, ocean, desert, volcano, and earthquake. The students must give a report on 2 of the topics. How many different selections of 2 topics are possible?

_____

D. Helen has 6 books in her backpack about the following topics: math, literature, history, plants, animals, and science fiction. Helen's mother told her she was allowed to bring 3 books to her grandmother's house. How many different selections of 3 books are possible?

_____

E. Scott, Brandon, and Nicki are running in a road race. If each finishes the race either in first, second, or third place, how many different ways are possible to finish the race?

_____

F. Franklin School is having a read-a-thon to raise money. April, Marie, Robert, and Carlos are the top 4 finalists. If first and second prizes are awarded among the 4 finalists, how many different ways are possible for first and second prizes to be awarded?

_____

G. Carolyn is taking Math, Science, Art, and Physical Education in the morning. If she is able to take these classes in any order, how many different schedules are possible?

_____

H. Heather is at the ice cream shop. There are 7 kinds of ice cream to choose from: rocky road, mint chocolate chip, butter pecan, chocolate, vanilla, strawberry, and cookie dough. If Heather gets 2 scoops of ice cream, each a different flavor, how many combinations of 2 scoops are possible?

_____

Name_____

Use the tables to solve the problems.

Students in Sports	
wrestling	13
track	20
soccer	25
tennis	25
volleyball	29
basketball	43
baseball	66
football	69

A. What is the mean of the students in sports?

_____

B. Which sports are nearest to the mean?

_____

C. What is the median of the students in sports?

_____

D. What is the mode of the students in sports?

_____

E. What is the range of the students in sports?

_____

F. What is the mean of the students in first-period classes?

_____

G. Which class is nearest this mean?

_____

H. What is the mode of the students in first-period classes?

_____

I. What is the median of the students in first-period classes?

_____

J. What is the range of the students in first-period classes?

_____

Students in First-Period Classes	
Art	29
Music	24
Physical Education	30
Science	27
Reading	21
Social Studies	24
Math	34

ANSWERS

Page 3
A. 12,585 acres
B. 6,204 tons
C. 2,925 bushels
D. 32 bouquets
E. 12,376 flats
F. 513,773 tons
G. 564,570 bushels

Page 4
A. $264.95
B. $2,010.51
C. $41,942.88
D. $79.95
E. 29 cents
F. $47.88
G. $2.70
H. $23.50

Page 5
A. $3\frac{1}{8}$ yards
B. $9\frac{3}{8}$ yards
C. $23\frac{1}{8}$ yards
D. $18\frac{11}{16}$ yards
E. $27\frac{1}{24}$ yards
F. $8\frac{7}{20}$ inches
G. $15\frac{2}{3}$ yards

Page 6
A. 50 inches
B. $2\frac{7}{16}$ feet
C. $4.56
D. 9 lights
E. 50 inches
F. 12 pieces
G. $\frac{4}{9}$
H. 3 stools

Page 7
A. x + 4
B. 62 − y
C. 15 − w
D. 82 − x
E. x + 15
F. y + 19
G. 5 × m
H. 65/x
I. 4 × k
J. y/25
K. 3 × d

Page 8
A. 33 + n = 78;
45 students in the Glee Club
B. n − 21 = 80;
101 students in the Drama Club
C. n + 4 = 23;
19 students in the band
D. n − 182 = 144;
326 students in the Dance Club
E. n + 70 = 214;
144 students in the Reading Club
F. n − $125 = $950;
$1,075 raised this year

Page 9
A. 11d = 5,599; 509 miles
B. d/72 = 3; 216 miles
C. 156 = 12k; 13 miles
D. d/60 = 2.5; 150 miles
E. 7d = 11,200; 1,600
F. 4d = 640; 160 miles
G. d/12 = 60; 720 miles
H. 175d = 700; 4 times

Page 10
A. 2n + 4 = 20; 8
B. n/11 − 2 = 1; 33
C. 3n + $2 = $20; $6
D. 8n + $450 = $2,250; $225
E. 8n + $25 = $145; $15
F. 6n − $25 = $227; $42
G. 7n + $5 = $47; $6

Page 11
A. 5 degrees
B. ⁻4° F
C. ⁻6° F
D. ⁻10° F
E. 20 degrees
F. ⁻1° F
G. 54 degrees

Page 12
A. ⁻25 yards
B. ⁻5 yards
C. 48 yards
D. ⁻10 yards
E. ⁻48 yards
F. 36 yards
G. ⁻5 yards

Page 13
A. 6n = ⁻18; ⁻3
B. n/⁻13 = ⁻4; 52
C. n + ⁻4 = ⁻7; ⁻3
D. n + ⁻13 = 1972; 1985
E. 8n = ⁻72; ⁻9
F. n − ⁻5 = ⁻5; ⁻10
G. n/2 = ⁻19; ⁻38

Page 14
A. $\frac{3}{8}$
B. $13\frac{1}{4}$
C. $3\frac{1}{8}$
D. $22\frac{9}{16}$
E. ⁻$1\frac{2}{5}$
F. $\frac{3}{4}$

Page 15
A. ⁻71.4 pounds
B. ⁻1.78 pounds
C. ⁻2 pounds
D. ⁻$5\frac{1}{2}$ pounds
E. ⁻3 pounds
F. $\frac{5}{12}$ gain
G. ⁻2.1 pounds

Page 16
A. $3 per hour
B. 45 words per minute
C. $1.75 per hour
D. $8.80
E. 3,360 kilometers
F. 37¢ per liter
G. 55 pages per hour
H. 64 minutes per class

© Frank Schaffer Publications, Inc.

ANSWERS

Page 17

A. seashell design cards—33¢ per card
floral design cards—37¢ per card
Seashell design

B. Top Quality Tapes—$2.97 per tape
Great Quality Tapes—$2.95 per tape
Great Quality Tapes

C. 32-ounce bottle—5¢ per ounce
64-ounce bottle—4¢ per ounce
The 64-ounce bottle

D. 1.5-ounce bottle—$29.30 per ounce
3-ounce bottle—$29.66 per ounce
The 1.5-ounce bottle

E. 3 socks—$2.54 a pair
2 socks—$2.64 a pair
The 3 socks

F. 5 cans—31¢ per can
3 cans—33¢ per can
The 5 cans

Page 18

A. $37/100 = n/215$; about 80 people
B. $2/3 = n/15$; 10 cups of punch mix
C. $1/13 = n/100$; 8 boxes
D. $2/\$5 = n/\$27.50$; 11 bouquets
E. $5/8 = n/200$; 125 people
F. $4/\$9 = 10/n$; $22.50

Page 19

A. $48
B. $36
C. $31.25
D. $19.50
E. $4.50
F. $291.50
G. $85.75

Page 20

A. $.25 \times n = 32$; 128
B. $.50 \times n = 190$; 380
C. $.65 \times n = 130$; 200
D. $.30 \times n = 90$; $300
E. $.35 \times n = 21$; 60
F. $.07 \times n = 42$; 600

Page 21

A. 45%
B. 225%
C. 87%
D. 500%
E. 55%
F. 20%
G. 70%
H. 20%

Page 22

A. $1,680
B. Interest—$3.093.75
Total—$10,593.75
C. $3,027.50
D. $1,029.60
E. Interest—$36
Total—$836
F. $200
G. $663.28

Page 23

A. 133 feet
B. 18 feet
C. 235.5 centimeters
D. 26.1 feet
E. 113.04 inches
F. 25 feet

Page 24

A. 13 feet
B. 192 square feet
C. 16.8 square feet; $235.03
D. 78.5 square feet
E. 29.2 square feet
F. 80.5 square feet

Page 25

A. 232 in.^{2}
B. 2,400 cm^2
C. 1,507.2 in.^{2}
D. 120 in.^{2}
E. 200.96 cm^2
F. 87.92 in.^{2}

Page 26

A. 276.2 cm^3
B. 4,032 in.^{3}
C. 5 in.^{3}
D. 286 cm^3
E. 5.2 m^3

Page 27

A. football–1/11; basketball–2/11
volleyball–3/11; soccer ball–5/11
B. medium shirt–3/17;
large shorts–2/17
C. red sweatshirt–7/18;
blue sweatshirt–4/18 or 2/9;
white sweatshirt–5/18;
yellow sweatshirt–2/18 or 1/9
D. blue baseball cap–3/18 or 1/6;
red baseball cap–9/18 or 1/2
E. 7/22

Page 28

A. about 52 tornadoes
B. about 284 rainy days
C. about 1 hurricane
D. about 146 rainy days
E. 3 floods
F. about 1 hurricane
G. 28 thunderstorms

Page 29

A. 24
B. 10
C. 10
D. 20
E. 6
F. 12
G. 24
H. 21

Page 30

A. 36 students
B. volleyball and basketball
C. 27 students
D. 25 students
E. 56 students
F. 27 students
G. science
H. 24 students
I. 27 students
J. 13 students

© Frank Schaffer Publications, Inc.